Green Smoothies

30 Easy and Delicious Green Smoothie Recipes to Boost Your Energy, Lose Weight and Revitalize Your Life

Sara Elliott Price

Published in The USA by:
Success Life Publishing
125 Thomas Burke Dr.
Hillsborough, NC 27278

Copyright © 2015 by Sara Elliott Price

ISBN-10: 151187175X

ALL RIGHTS RESERVED. No part of this publication may be reproduced or transmitted in any form whatsoever, electronic, or mechanical, including photocopying, recording, or by any informational storage or retrieval system without the express written permission from the author, except for the use of brief quotations in a book review.

Disclaimer

Every effort has been made to accurately represent this book and its potential. Results vary with every individual, and your results may or may not be different from those depicted. No promises, guarantees or warranties, whether stated or implied, have been made that you will produce any specific result from this book. Your efforts are individual and unique, and may vary from those shown. Your success depends on your efforts, background and motivation.

The material in this publication is provided for educational and informational purposes only and is not intended as medical advice. The information contained in this book should not be used to diagnose or treat any illness, metabolic disorder, disease or health problem. Always consult your physician or health care provider before beginning any nutrition or exercise program. Use of the programs, advice, and information contained in this book is at the sole choice and risk of the reader.

Table Of Contents

Introduction

Chapter 1: What are Green Smoothies? 3

Chapter 2: Green Smoothies to Revitalize Your Health . 8

Chapter 3: Making Green Smoothies You'll Love 11

Chapter 4: 30 Delicious Green Smoothie Recipes 16

    Kale, Lemon and Ginger 17

    Cucumber, Nutmeg and Apple 18

    De-Bloating Smoothie 19

    Vanilla Lime Green Smoothie 20

    Green Tea Smoothie 21

    Kiwi and Spinach Smoothie 22

    Pure Green Smoothie 23

    Spinach and Peanut Butter Smoothie 24

    Avocado Green Smoothie 25

    The Island Blast 26

    Creamy Green Smoothie 27

    Tropical Cleanse 28

    Spinach and Avocado Smoothie 29

    Berry Green Smoothie 30

    Banana, Spinach and Pineapple Smoothie 31

    Holly's Green Smoothie Recipe 32

    Strawberries and Kale Green Smoothie 33

    Green Raspberry Smoothie 34

Kale and Pineapple Green Smoothies 35
Chocolate Mint Green Smoothie 36
Simple Green Smoothie 37
Green Fruit Smoothie 38
Cranberry-Kale Smoothie 39
Cherry, Apple, Beet Smoothie 40
Melon-Cucumber Green Smoothie 41
Orange-Pomegranate Green Smoothie 42
Pineapple-Celery Green Smoothie 43
Pear-Raspberry with Beet 44
Green Strawberry-Kiwi Lemonade 45
Summer Splash 46

Chapter 5: How to "Boost" Your Smoothies 47
Hemp Seeds 49
Chia Seeds 49
Green Superfood Powders 50
Maca 50
Coconut Oil 51

Conclusion 52

Introduction

I want to thank you for purchasing, *"Green Smoothies: 30 Easy and Delicious Green Smoothie Recipes to Boost Your Energy, Lose Weight and Revitalize Your Life!"*

By deciding to pick up this book you are now well on your way to becoming the healthiest version of yourself and achieving the energy, vibrancy and happiness you've always dreamed of.

Throughout this book you will discover why green smoothies may be your greatest weapon to becoming healthier than you have ever been. Not only will you get healthy, you will also lose the weight you have been trying to get rid of for years!

As we all know, proper nutrition is the foundation for a healthy lifestyle. Green smoothies can give you that nutrition in a very delicious way! The word 'disease' doesn't have to be in your future and even if you have a disease right now there is a good chance that the goodness locked inside fresh fruits and veggies can heal you from the inside out.

Are you ready to wake up with bursting energy and a clear complexion? How about a pep in your step with no more pain? Or maybe you just want to regain a little youth, lose a few pounds and halt the aging process. It doesn't matter what health goals you are after because green smoothies can take you there. All you need to do is follow the advice in this book and I promise only good things can come from it.

Today most people take a pill for everything or look for some magic potion that will solve all their health issues. Most people don't understand that the healing starts from within. Quit giving your body the bad stuff and feed it the stuff it needs and you will start to thrive. Most people never know what true health feels like. They go through life feeling "OK" but I want you to feel **AWESOME**! The nutrition from fresh produce is the key to all the health goals and dreams you have set for yourself.

Jumpstart your health by jumping head first into the following pages. If you read the information, understand it and apply it in your daily life I have no doubts you will feel like a brand new, better version of yourself a month from now.

Thanks again for downloading this book, I hope it serves you well on your health journey.

Chapter 1:

What are Green Smoothies?

If you're like most people, you can't help but to smile expectantly when you hear the word 'smoothies' and that's no surprise because you know you are in for a real treat, right?

As for green smoothies, however, some people grimace in fear expecting it to taste reminiscent of swamp water. The fact of the matter remains that no matter how health conscious you are, it is a whole lot easier to drink your veggies than it is to eat them. And do you know the absolute best part about green smoothies? They all taste fantastic, believe it or not and you don't have to spend tons of your hard-earned dollars buying a juicer to enable you to prepare them. You can simply use your good ol' blender and churn up those leafy greens really well.

Now I know if you had a nickel for every time you heard how healthy vegetables are, you would probably be rich, but at the risk of sounding repetitive, you do need your veggies. I don't expect you to jump on the bandwagon just because veggies *are* actually good for you because let's face it, it is often hard to do things that are good for us.

Even though you are probably tempted to turn up your nose at the notion of blending green veggies into a smoothie, you should know that in addition to being good for your health, these veggies (especially the combinations listed in the recipes below) are so good for everything from your skin, to your blood pressure, to your eyes, to your hair, to your internal organs, to your memory and yes, your weight!

Now extolling all the virtues of vegetables would be next to impossible because they are numerous and frankly unquantifiable, but in the end, it is enough to know that green smoothies are packed with so many healthy vitamins, minerals and other nutrients that it's often best to include them in your diet and make it a daily practice. Most green smoothies often have kale and spinach as their chief ingredient probably because they give green smoothies that amazing color and also come packed with calcium, protein and iron.

Most dieticians and other experts have expressed a preference for green smoothies over juicing because with juices, the fiber content is often extracted and if you have ever had a bad case of constipation then I assume you know how important fiber is to the body. Also, green smoothies are a more reliable source of energy, can be low in calories, tastier and infinitely more filling than juices.

The first time I heard about how fantastic green smoothies

tasted, I thought it was a sales pitch especially since the person talking about it at the time was a dietician. However, the first time I reluctantly took a sip, I was so amazed at the taste I actually drank *two* glasses and became a convert for life!

Green smoothies are fast becoming as common as bottled water since they can often be seen clutched in the hands of everyone from celebrities to working people but some people are still at a loss as to what green smoothies actually are.

Green smoothies are smoothies made by blending fresh, green leafy vegetables with equally fresh fruits. The green vegetables are the main ingredients though, and the fruits are often merely added to make the smoothies taste great. Some people try using juicers but the thing is, with juicers you get juices; green smoothies can only be made using your blender and most times, we recommend high-powered blenders. Blenders are a better choice for preparing green smoothies because they tend to retain the fiber content of the veggies and fruits used, unlike juicers which separate the juice from the pulp.

Green smoothies work wonders for people looking to shed a few pounds (yes the weight does drop off even without hours of cardio). Green smoothies are the next best thing in nutrition and the best part is, green smoothies are made from fresh, raw vegetables which mean your body gets exposed to the huge amounts of nutrients without any preservatives, flavors, etc.

Now some experts like Dr. Ann Wigmore would tell you "consuming chlorophyll is like receiving a healthy blood transfusion." Green smoothies are the world's shortest route to consuming a mix of healthy vitamins and nutrients that can only be received from raw vegetables. Come on, even being a vegetarian isn't the easiest choice in the world, but green smoothies make it so much easier.

Some people wouldn't even touch a raw vegetable with a ten-foot pole to save their lives, but the good news is that green smoothies afford every single person the opportunity to get all the nutrients from the greens without so much as tasting the green veggies. With green smoothies, you can consume as many healthy greens as you need to without developing an unhealthy loathing for mealtimes.

Green smoothies are fast becoming a lifestyle choice for most people because they are so delicious, affordable and you can make them at home yourself quickly and easily.

Most moms will tell you that they have devised hundreds of ways to slip veggies into their kids', husbands' and even their own food without anyone picking up on the taste of the veggies. Unfortunately, you can't hide the taste of vegetables in most traditional ways of cooking. Surprisingly though, with green smoothies, the taste of the vegetables never comes through which means you get to give your body the nutrients it needs without having to make your taste buds suffer in the process.

A friend once laughingly referred to green smoothies as a 'surprise in a cup' and she was right. We have been practically brainwashed from childhood into assuming that anything green has got to be bitter. In fact, some people wouldn't let a piece of green bubble gum anywhere near their mouth because they half expect it to taste like raw vegetables. But green smoothies are another story—the first sip is always an amazement, as you suddenly realize that no one was trying to trick you. They are a delight to the taste buds and I guarantee you won't be disappointed.

Chapter 2:
Green Smoothies to Revitalize Your Health

Green smoothies are a miracle of nature for detoxification and before you race for the hills, this does not mean you have to starve, suffer and go without food. Green smoothies are like good health in a glass. The chlorophyll content in green produce is out of this world which often combines with the fiber for a balanced detox that will have your doctor grinning from ear to ear.

The high fiber content in green smoothies also does wonders for the colon. The green smoothies are also responsible for improved immune system function and also liver and kidney function. Not to mention it also does wonders for the digestive system. Green smoothies contain minerals, fiber, antioxidants, polyphenols, water, vitamins—and the list goes on!

Green smoothies are remarkably easy to digest because the blending breaks down the cell walls where the nutrients are encased and so the body absorbs them easier than in their whole state.

In case you didn't know, some people are unable to chew their food and if they also suffer from low hydrochloric acid, they eventually stop enjoying green veggies and even develop an outright dislike for them. This is bad because it becomes a vicious circle of sorts given the fact that stomach acids are necessary for digestion especially when it comes to greens.

People who do not eat greens become deficient in the nutrients which create stomach acids which means they lack the ability to digest greens properly. Green smoothies are just about the only way to trick your body into taking whole greens and digesting them effortlessly.

Green smoothies flush out toxic waste faster than anything you could imagine, plus they also take care of cravings and satisfy actual hunger. Yep, believe it or not!

The best thing about green smoothies is that they don't have to be one of those seasonal foods. You can totally enjoy them all year round especially since green vegetables can easily be grown in your own backyard.

Another benefit of consuming green smoothies is that not only are you increasing your daily produce intake, you're also getting much needed hydration. During a normal meal where food is cooked, the water is evaporated, but in a green smoothie all that fresh juice is kept intact within your smoothie. This means less worry about reaching your daily water quota!

Most people believe that it's so hard to eat healthy. They think it takes hours to prepare, cook and clean up the mess of a healthy meal. Smoothies, however, defy this belief! They are incredibly easy and simple to prepare and take only a few minutes. Just toss your ingredients in your blender and bam! You have a delicious meal that's easy to take with you on the go.

Say goodbye to your multi-vitamin. Smoothies contain such a vast array of nutrients that they put those hard, un-absorbable tablets to shame. You will get instant energy and health benefits from drinking a smoothie, whereas with your multivitamin you may never get some of the advertised "benefits" at all.

One major benefit of smoothies is that they can be tailored to fit a vast array of health needs. From inflammation, to diabetes, to weight loss and everything in between. You can create a delicious smoothie that can help you begin healing your problems without even having to visit the doctor's office. With smoothies, you can finally take your health into your own hands!

Chapter 3:
Making Green Smoothies You'll Love

Now don't dash off to try any of these delicious recipes without taking time to learn how to make your own green smoothie. These steps will ensure that it tastes as great as it should and also gives your body the nutrition it needs to heal itself, revitalize, detox and even fight illnesses.

Here are a few steps you should keep in mind when preparing green smoothies.

Add liquid

Before blending your ingredients into a healthy, delicious green smoothie, make certain to add some liquid before blending. This makes it easier and not quite so thick.

You could use water as a liquid, or you could use coconut water, fresh squeezed fruit juices, or even nut milks (my personal favorite being almond). They make it easier for the blades of your blender to chop up the veggies and they make your smoothie that much easier to sip.

Use fruits to enhance the taste of your smoothie

Hey, those fruits pack their own unique nutritional punch and if you can't down one of those healthy greens without making a face, then you should definitely add fruits to the mix.

Even if you are one of those people who can chug down bland, evil-smelling, completely green vegetable drinks without making a face, you should try throwing in fruits. Experts often advise that you use two or more fruits in a green smoothie blend. More often than not, banana goes wonderfully with strawberry; mangoes with pineapple; pear with orange; and apple with blueberry. For green smoothies, your aim should be 60% fruits and 40% greens; it tastes better all-around and also helps you sneak healthy greens into you and your family's diet.

Think of your blender

Yes, I know it's an inanimate object and probably doesn't require much consideration from you, but in truth, unless you use high-end blenders like Vitamix or Blendtec you really should chop up your veggies before blending them. No need to dice them all up completely, just chop them. And even if you do use these high end blenders, you still need to chop up larger fruits before blending them to make it a faster process.

Take spinach over kale for beginners

Kale is right up there with the heavy-weights when it comes to nutrients from greens but if you are new to the green smoothie lifestyle, you might want to start out with spinach first. It packs quite a nutritional punch, but it may not be as nutritious as kale which probably accounts for why it tastes slightly better. Spinach is used in a lot of recipes but you could easily replace the spinach with kale if you are feeling adventurous.

Use ice cubes

Smoothies are meant to be savored and enjoyed — green or no — which is why the best way to make them is with ice cubes. Trust me, as delicious as green smoothies are, they taste even better with ice cubes thrown in for a real chilling effect. Another easier alternative is to use frozen fruits in your smoothie which adds to the creamy texture and makes your smoothie more like a milkshake.

Take it slow

Green smoothies, delicious as they are, have to be treated like most diets: slow and steady. Most green smoothies are tasty but you still want to ease into it and not start a crash diet. Your best bet for sticking to green smoothies as a dieting plan is to start slow and make it a habit.

Observe basic hygiene

Food poisoning is not a word your doctor dreamt up and unfortunately it is a whole lot easier to get food poisoning from raw fruits and vegetables than it is from cooked foods.

Green smoothies may be the world's healthiest meal, but you have to remember to wash your fruits and veggies properly *before* you so much as throw them in the blender. Also, make certain to always wash your blender after preparing your green smoothie.

No matter how delicious your green smoothie is, try to finish it up all at once. Some people often refrigerate any extra after preparation and take the second helping a few hours later; that's ok too, but more often than not, the green smoothie is best consumed as soon as it is made.

Servings

You should know that the quantities recommended for each ingredient in the green smoothie recipes are not cast in stone; you could reduce or increase it to suit whatever serving size you had in mind. Please note though, that the general recommended ratio for green smoothies is 60% fruits and 40% veggies but for beginners, the recommended ratio is 70% fruits and 30% veggies until they have adjusted to the new diet.

Change recipes

When it comes to green smoothies, variety is indeed the spice of life. You should change up and explore as many of the recommended recipes as you can because it not only exposes you to many essential nutrients, it also makes it harder for you to get bored with the taste of any one particular green smoothie.

Chapter 4:
30 Delicious Green Smoothie Recipes

So here's the moment we've all been waiting for…recipes! If you have ever tried green smoothies then you know that they often sound good in theory but more often than not taste so horrible that it's all you can do not to boil your tongue after spitting out the first sip.

Well if this has been your constant experience, then I am willing to bet you had the worst recipes possible. There are some green smoothies guaranteed to work wonders on your health, weight and general well-being and yet they taste amazing—like actual delicious smoothies. Here are some of those recipes for your tasty, healthy, green smoothie diet.

Kale, Lemon and Ginger

Lemon is a great cleansing and detoxifying ingredient. It contains properties that are very active in reducing anxiety and depression. Lemon detoxifies like you wouldn't believe. Kale has been recognized as one of the highest sources of minerals on the planet among other amazing health benefits.

For this recipe, you need to have the following:

- 1 C water
- ½ a lemon, already peeled and seeded
- 1 lime peeled and seeded
- 1 C packed kale
- ½ Tablespoon of grated peeled ginger

Cucumber, Nutmeg and Apple

This is a comfort smoothie with the ability to take care of your sweet tooth and also fill you up from lunch time to dinner. Nutmeg has strong antibacterial properties and has also been thought to be good for the heart. It also contains myristicin which is thought to inhibit development of Alzheimer's and improve memory.

The phytonutrients in apples have been shown to help reduce blood sugar and as for your cucumber, they are an amazing source of Vitamin B.

The ingredients for this smoothie include:

- 1 C water
- A handful of spinach (be sure to remove the stems)
- 1 small cucumber
- 1 apple
- 1/8 teaspoon of ground nutmeg
- ½ a lime (make certain you peel)

De-Bloating Smoothie

This smoothie does exactly what the name suggests; it helps de-bloat your achy stomach and makes room for your airways. Banana is a good source of potassium and also helps to regulate your sodium levels, while pineapple and coconut milk have diuretic properties that help flush excess water.

The ingredients for this include:

- 1 medium banana
- 1 C strawberries
- 1/4 of a medium sized pineapple
- 2 handfuls of fresh spinach
- ¼ C coconut milk

Vanilla Lime Green Smoothie

If you think you have tasted all green smoothies have to offer, then you are sadly mistaken. The vanilla lime green smoothie is famous for its tangy citrus taste and I guarantee that if you taste it just once, you could easily become hooked.

Here's what you need:

- 1 banana
- 1 lime (peeled and seeded)
- ½ teaspoon of vanilla extract
- 1 good handful of spinach leaves
- ½ C ice
- 2 teaspoons of honey
- ½ C vanilla yogurt
- 2 Tablespoons almond milk

Green Tea Smoothie

The green tea smoothie tastes much better than you may expect. Packed with grapes, spinach and banana, you'll find tons of cleansing and weight loss properties from each sip. This unique mix of ingredients moves through your system flushing your body in a way that is guaranteed to make you feel like a million bucks.

The ingredients are:

- 1 ½ C green grapes
- 1 C baby spinach
- 2 bananas
- 1 C green tea
- Ice cubes

Kiwi and Spinach Smoothie

This smoothie is a delight to the taste buds and you absolutely will not taste the spinach, just lots of sweetness that tastes more like a kiwi surprise than anything else.

The ingredients are:

- 2 kiwi fruit, peeled and halved
- 1 banana
- ½ an apple (cored)
- 2 handfuls of baby spinach (or kale)
- 2 Tablespoons of flaxseed (flaxseed is optional)
- ½ C Greek vanilla yogurt

Pure Green Smoothie

The pure green smoothie has a tropical taste because of the inclusion of juicy mangoes in the mix. The pineapple in this smoothie contains bromelain, which helps to treat indigestion and inflammation. So, if you're having stomach pain or digestive issues this is the smoothie for you.

The pure green smoothie includes:

- 1 C plain yogurt
- ¼ of a medium sized pineapple
- ½ a fresh mango
- 2 or 3 handfuls of spinach (or collards)
- 1 Tablespoon of chia seeds

Spinach and Peanut Butter Smoothie

This smoothie will make your taste buds do a wild dance and yet works wonders for your body. This is my current favorite after workout snack. High in protein, good fats and delicious.

The ingredients you need are:

- 2 C spinach
- 1 C vanilla almond milk
- 1 C plain Greek yogurt
- 1 Tablespoon of pure, undiluted honey
- 1 Tablespoon of peanut butter
- 1 scoop of chocolate protein powder
- 1 Tablespoon Chia seeds
- 2 cups of ice

<u>Avocado Green Smoothie</u>

Have you ever tried to get kids to eat vegetables or watched someone try? If you are one of those people who regard green smoothies with all the trepidation reserved for crawly things like spiders, then this is one drink you should definitely try. Trust me, even kids would ask for seconds.

The ingredients are:

- ¼ of a medium sized pineapple
- ½ of a whole avocado (remove the seed)
- ¼ C pineapple juice
- 2 handfuls of fresh spinach
- 1 Tablespoon of flaxseed (optional)
- 1 banana

The Island Blast

The exotic name may make you sit up and take notice, but the best part is, it not only tastes fantastic but it's also very nutritious, does wonders for your waistline and your general health. Seriously, if you are looking to lose weight, look no further.

The ingredients you need are:

- 1 medium sized banana
- 1 celery stalk
- ¼ of a cucumber
- ¼ of a medium sized pineapple
- 1 small handful of parsley
- A little bit of ginger (to taste)
- ¼ of a whole coconut (be sure to dice it up)

Creamy Green Smoothie

Simple, creamy and sweet. The carotenoids in spinach are wonderful for the eyes and the avocado is a natural source of healthy fat.

The ingredients needed are:

- 1 avocado
- 1 small banana
- 1 orange (peeled and seeded)
- A handful of spinach
- 1 C unsweetened vanilla almond milk

Tropical Cleanse

A very simple and easy to prepare green smoothie with fairly common ingredients. The ginger gives the smoothie a tangy, sharp, spicy flavor while providing a super anti-inflammatory boost.

Blend the following ingredients:

- ¼ of a whole, fresh pineapple
- 1 small banana
- 1 finger of ginger
- 2 handfuls of spinach
- 1 C coconut water

Spinach and Avocado Smoothie

As with most other smoothies, you could easily replace the spinach with kale or collard. This smoothie helps you increase your intake of water, which as you know is very good for you. The ingredients are thankfully common and easy to find at your local produce store.

Simply blend together the following:

- 2 handfuls of spinach
- 1 apple (no need to peel but be sure to core and chop)
- ½ of a whole avocado
- ¼ C water
- 1 C apple juice (if desired)

Berry Green Smoothie

This green smoothie is a personal favorite and in case you haven't guessed, raspberries and blueberries together make an amazing combination. The best part is, berries have more antioxidants than almost any other fresh fruit or vegetable.

The ingredients you need for this are:

- 2 handfuls of spinach leaves
- ½ C blueberries
- ½ C raspberries
- ½ C almond milk
- 1 ripe banana
- 2 tablespoons of oats

Banana, Spinach and Pineapple Smoothie

Spinach is truly wondrous. It eases constipation and amongst other things protects the mucus lining of the stomach which helps keep you free from stomach ulcers. And if that isn't incentive enough, you should know that the nutrient composition of spinach makes for a beautiful complexion.

Blend these ingredients together:

- ½ C coconut milk
- 2 - 3 handfuls of spinach
- ¼ of a medium sized pineapple
- 1 ripe banana

Holly's Green Smoothie Recipe

The trick to this particular green smoothie is not to go overboard with the greens. If you like spicy lemonade, you'll really enjoy this recipe.

Here's what you need:

- 1 finger of fresh peeled ginger
- ¼ of a lemon
- 1 or 2 cored apples, unpeeled
- 5 stalks of kale with the stem removed
- 1 avocado
- A few ounces of water
- Ice cubes

Strawberries and Kale Green Smoothie

Kale is a popular choice that easily replaces spinach because as nutritious as spinach is, kale packs more of a nutritional punch. Kale is high in iron, full of antioxidants, Vitamin K, Vitamin C, fiber, sulfur, and in fact, more calcium than milk. Several people go on a green smoothie diet with emphasis on kale and in a mere month they have lost pounds and pounds of fat and excess weight.

Blend the following together to prepare:

- 1 C strawberry
- 1 handful of kale
- 1 C vanilla almond milk
- 1 banana
- Ice cubes

Green Raspberry Smoothie

This is one of the healthiest green smoothies you could make. Ripe raspberries are extremely high in antioxidants and have phytonutrients like ellagitannins that have been shown to help kill cancer cells. This is done by sending signals that prompt the cancer cells to begin a cycle of programmed death known as apoptosis.

The ingredients are:

- 1 apple (cored but unpeeled)
- 1 handful of lettuce
- ¼ C soaked pumpkin seeds
- ½ C water
- 1 Tablespoon of flax seeds
- 1 celery stalk
- ½ C raspberries
- Ice cubes

Kale and Pineapple Green Smoothies

Kale helps lower cholesterol, is high in iron and contains a ton of vitamin C. Add in the other ingredients and you have an excellent source of trace minerals, manganese, Vitamin B1, Vitamin B6, fiber, folate and pantothenic acid.

The ingredients you need are:

- ½ C coconut milk
- 2 C stemmed and chopped kale or spinach
- 2/3 of a medium sized pineapple
- 1 ripe banana
- Ice cubes

Chocolate Mint Green Smoothie

A low sugar, high protein, balanced meal. This delicious chocolate mint shake tastes more like a treat than a healthy meal. Chocolate is known as one of the best sources of antioxidants in the world. Add in the healthy fat, protein and greens and this smoothie could very well rival any healthy meal you could think of.

The necessary ingredients are:

- 3 handfuls of spinach
- 1 C unsweetened almond milk
- ½ an avocado
- 1 scoop of chocolate protein powder
- ½ a handful of fresh mint leaves
- 1 Tablespoon of dark chocolate chips or cacao nibs
- Stevia
- Ice cubes

Simple Green Smoothie

This smoothie might be simple, but it packs a huge nutritional punch. The best part is all these ingredients are very easy to get at any grocery store.

The ingredients you need for this are:

- 1 large orange (without peel)
- 1 banana
- 6 large strawberries
- 3 handfuls of spinach
- 1/3 cup of plain Greek yogurt
- 1 cup of ice

Green Fruit Smoothie

Looking for a great breakfast smoothie? Look no further! When you add almond milk and banana together you get a huge energy and protein boost depending on the source of nut milk. Mango is also very high in Vitamin E, which not only makes your skin look great but drastically increases your libido as well.

The ingredients needed are:

- 1 C spinach
- 1 C almond milk
- ½ C mango
- ½ C pineapple
- 1 banana

Cranberry-Kale Smoothie

Did someone scream the word 'happy'? If so, it could be they've been drinking this smoothie. The cranberries have compounds that improve moods and boost cognitive functions. This smoothie is great for relieving stress, anxiety and depression.

Blend the following ingredients:

- ½ C cranberries
- ½ C blueberries
- 1 banana
- 1 C frozen baby kale
- 8 oz. coconut water

Cherry, Apple, Beet Smoothie

If you need an inflammation fighting smoothie, then this is the recipe for you. The juice found in cherries reduces muscle inflammation and soreness after a workout which will help prevent lactic acid build up and help your recovery time.

Gather the following ingredients:

- ½ C cherries, pitted
- ¼ C beet, chopped
- ½ apple, cored
- 1 C beet greens (or baby kale)
- ¼ C pineapple
- 4 oz. almond milk

Melon-Cucumber Green Smoothie

If you're trying to kick toxins out of your life, then give this smoothie a go! Dandelions are extremely anti-inflammatory and improve liver function by removing toxins and balancing electrolytes. This is good news for anyone trying to detox or cleanse their body.

Here are the ingredients:

- 1 C honeydew melon
- 3 mint leaves
- ¼ cucumber with peel
- ½ frozen banana
- 1 teaspoon lime juice
- 1 ½ C dandelion greens
- 4 oz. almond milk

Orange-Pomegranate Green Smoothie

This smoothie is just plain delicious! Don't underestimate its health properties. Collard leaves are one of the best sources of plant-based calcium out there, meaning this smoothie can lead to stronger bones and teeth. Your cells will communicate better and your hormone levels will be kept in check. So go on, have a swig—nourish your immune system!

Use these ingredients:

- ½ pear, cored
- 1 orange (peeled and seeded)
- ¼ C pomegranate seeds
- 1 ½ collard leaves (no stems)
- 1 oz. water (if needed)

Pineapple-Celery Green Smoothie

Get ready for a blood transfusion because parsley is here! Parsley is one of the greatest sources of chlorophyll which is very similar to human blood. Chlorophyll is literally like drinking liquid sunlight. This smoothie will not only energize you, it will also help oxygenize your blood.

Gather the following ingredients:

- 1 banana
- ½ C pineapple
- 1 stalk celery
- ¼ C flat leaf parsley
- 1 ½ C greens (kale, spinach, collards, etc.)
- 4 oz. almond milk

Pear-Raspberry with Beet

If you're worried about your heart, worry no more. This could be just what the doctor ordered. Oats contain certain antioxidants that prevent free radicals from damaging cholesterol, which means the cholesterol you consume doesn't have to be as big a concern as you thought.

As a side note, spinach contains oxalic acid that blocks absorption of calcium and iron, but by pairing foods high in Vitamin C with spinach this is no longer a concern.

Here's what you'll need:

- ½ C beet, chopped
- 1 pear, cored
- ¼ C old fashioned oats
- ½ C raspberries
- 2 C spinach
- 8 oz. water

Green Strawberry-Kiwi Lemonade

If you don't ever want to get sick again, drink this daily. The fruits in this smoothie contain extremely high amounts of vitamin C. Not only that, but this smoothie is very alkaline based—meaning it can help flush out some of those harmful acids that have accumulated in your body. Even the tiny kiwi has the power to protect your DNA from oxidative stress and damage.

You will need the following ingredients:

- 1 kiwi, peeled
- ¾ C strawberries
- ¼ C pineapple
- ½ lemon (peeled and seeded)
- 2 C spinach
- 1 ½ C coconut water

Summer Splash

You may have never even heard of bok choy, but don't let that keep you from trying this smoothie recipe! Bok choy is from the cabbage family, meaning it contains a large amount of sulfuric compounds that have the potential to stop development of hormone sensitive cancers. Not only that, but the lutein it contains also protects your eyesight. So grab a glass and have a sip of this surprisingly refreshing recipe!

For this simple recipe the ingredients are:

- 2 C bok choy
- 2 C almond milk
- 1 C strawberries
- 2 C diced peaches

Chapter 5:
How to "Boost" Your Smoothies

Green smoothies are very attractive for people who are busy, because they are so easy and fast to prepare. A bonus is that, more often than not, they satisfy hunger and cravings for quite a while. You can prepare green smoothies and take them on the go or you can prepare and refrigerate the extras.

Green smoothies are the easiest way to consume your veggies because they are often so incredibly tasty that you do not have to 'bribe' yourself or your kids to drink them. In fact, don't be surprised if they go back for seconds.

You can also add or remove ingredients easily to suit your needs and stay confident knowing that whatever you have added will provide wonderful nutrients to your body.

Green smoothies are the best bet for anyone looking to have a healthier body, prevent disease and even boost the immune system because nothing you eat will ever truly be as healthy as fresh foods straight from Mother Nature!

Although green smoothies are a great way to detox and add fruits and veggies to your diet, they can also be "boosted" to create a more balanced meal. There is nothing wrong with making a plain fruit and leafy greens smoothie for breakfast, lunch or anytime but for some people that isn't enough sustenance. For these people you simply need to add in some fat and protein and you will feel like your green smoothie has become a serious meal.

In fact, unless you are trying to do a serious detox or are using green smoothies as simple snacks I suggest you consider adding in some fats and proteins and replacing your actual meals with smoothies. This is not only good for your health it's also a great way to save on time.

The macronutrients fat and protein aren't the only things you can "boost" in your green smoothies. While you're at it you can take your smoothies to a whole new level by adding in all sorts of super food and green powders. Even certain spices such as cinnamon are great for your health yet can also taste great in a green smoothie.

Fats and Proteins are great additions to any green smoothie. It's almost like they become complete. Without them your smoothie will never last you as long and your appetite will be growling for food within a couple of hours. In this book I'm not going to provide you with an exhaustive list of supplements—only the ones that I feel will benefit you the most.

Some of my favorite additions to green smoothies are the following.

Hemp Seeds

If there were 1 single thing I would want to always add into my smoothies, hemp seeds would be it. These wonderful seeds are loaded with all sorts of awesome nutrients. They are very high in protein and high in omega 3 fatty acids. The mineral content is even on par with some of the greens you put in your smoothies. These little seeds will even add a nice creamy texture to your smoothie.

Chia Seeds

These little seeds are more than what their cheesy infomercials would have you believe. The nutritional benefits of adding chia seeds to your smoothies are numerous. For starters, there are more omega-3's in a 1 oz. serving of chia seeds than there are in a serving of salmon! And if that isn't enough for you, a single serving of chia seeds contains a third of the fiber you need in an entire day and 25% of a large portion of your nutrients—including calcium, manganese and phosphorous. Add in the fact that there are 4.4 g of protein in a serving and this one addition to your smoothies can make them a complete and satisfying meal!

Green Superfood Powders

If you are really looking to drastically increase the nutritional value of your green smoothies, then green superfood powders are a must. These powders are loaded with tons of different compounds from plants that have the ability to strengthen, detoxify, and heal your body. You will find a vast array of superfood plants such as spirulina, chlorella and many different types of green vegetables. These are usually dried at a cool temperature to keep the enzymes intact. Simply adding the recommended serving of one of these powders to your daily smoothie is an easy way to get much needed nutrients into your diet without consuming as many vegetables.

Maca

This supplement is best consumed with your smoothie in its gelatinized powder form. This aids in easier digestion, as the maca powder is slightly heated to prevent the ill effects of consuming it raw. Maca is a tuber, just like the potato, meaning you can become sick from consuming it in its raw state. Maca powder is very high in minerals that you can't easily get elsewhere. What truly makes this plant special is its energetic and libido enhancing properties. Just one teaspoon a day is all you need in your smoothie to see the positive benefits it has to offer.

Coconut Oil

This has to be my favorite healthy fat source! I use it not just in my smoothies raw, but also for cooking and baking and even as a moisturizer, believe it or not. As an added benefit, coconut oil provides antibacterial and antimicrobial properties. Coconut oil is also a wonderful addition to your smoothie if you're looking for clean burning energy that will keep you going strong for hours. The medium-chain triglycerides also aid in weight loss since they give you increased energy, thus giving you more of a daily calorie burn.

I use these five supplements almost on a daily basis in my smoothies. There are many other wonderful additions you can put in your smoothies, such as: goji powder, acai powder, camu camu, cacao, flax seeds, the list goes on. Just know that the most important part of a smoothie are the fresh fruits and vegetables. Try not to get too caught up in or overwhelmed by adding extras—it definitely isn't necessary. However, when you're ready, adding supplements to your smoothies can take your health to a whole new level.

Conclusion

Thank you for taking the time to read this book. You can reach all your health goals and dreams by simply learning and applying new healthy lifestyle choices.

If you take the information you've learned in this book and actually put it into practice, you will succeed in your health and healing journey. Whether your goal is to be free of pain, lose some weight or become younger you **can** do it!

With the strategies and green smoothie recipes you now have, you are definitely on the right path to success. I wish you all the best and many years of health and happiness.

Remember; never stop learning how to become the healthiest version of yourself. You owe it to yourself to feel what true health and vibrancy really is. Health is a lifelong passion everyone should pursue. The easiest way to do this is simply pick up a new book every month and apply what you find useful. Doing this makes even the largest health obstacles seem small and gives a deep level of hope.

If you would like to learn more about losing weight with smoothies be sure to check out my book 'Weight Loss Smoothies: 33 Healthy and Delicious Smoothie Recipes to Boost Your Metabolism, Burn Fat and Lose Weight Fast.'

Made in the USA
Middletown, DE
26 January 2018